Table of Contents

1. Introduction
2. Feeling confined
3. Working in adolescent residential programs
4. Knowing what's not for you
5. Staying balanced: sleep
6. Staying balanced: TV and vacation
7. Fix it or leave it alone
8. Eat well and use the restroom
9. Respect my time off
10. Stress kills
11. Toxic friends and difficult conversations
12. Sexual harassment & monitoring phone calls
13. The lion's den
14. Supervisors needing supervision
15. Residential programs
16. Escaping legal persecution
17. Secondary gain
18. Violating patient rights
19. Transferring patients
20. Grievances and star cards
21. Abuse, neglect or exploitation
22. Program schedules
23. Psychiatrists
24. Pastoral counselors and cab drivers
25. Reward for behavioral problems
26. Professionals behaving badly

27. Right to privacy
28. Assisted living facilities & outpatient
29. Audits and language barriers
30. Concluding remarks for consumers
31. Tips for providers

Introduction

Water, depicted on this book’s cover, can sustain life but too much of it can cause drowning. Oftentimes a person really can’t decipher the depth of a body of water until they actually get into it. But as you wade in the water, you’ll discover things aren’t always as they seem; there maybe something menacing lurking underneath the surface.

I’m leaving in worst shape than I did before I sought your help! Has that thought ever crossed your mind? It surely has with me after I’ve received healthcare services! While serving as a provider of mental health/substance abuse treatment services, I’ve had the intention of helping others but have come to the realization that sometimes the help I offered was not enough. The help I gave wasn’t what they needed, but what I or the agency felt they should have. Ever felt that doctors, counselors, nurses, technicians were more interested in your ability to pay for services than helping you?

My intention for writing this book is to increase awareness for patients/clients, families, courts, and clinicians by disclosing my learning experiences. Hopefully, my shared learning experiences will serve as a resource guide that allows individuals the opportunity to make a more informed choice before engaging in the behavioral health system. In addition, I strive to provide clinical providers with valuable knowledge and revelations that will hopefully make the mental health/substance abuse treatment services better. I hope to offer support for providers who are frustrated in this profession. There is a huge difference in helping people in general versus helping people in need especially when the clinician has to meet those needs with very limited time, resources, and minimal support from management.

Part I: Advice for Healthcare Providers

Feeling confined by this profession

Working with populations that live in the same segment of the city as you can be nerve-wrecking. I was hoping that the only time I would see some clients were during working hours at the job. However, if you know anything about working in social services, the income you make oftentimes puts you in the same neighborhood with the clients you serve. Working in rural areas is the most difficult, especially if you were born and raised there.

Serving as a children's case manager, I would pass by several houses of clients that lived near my grandma's house. Sometimes, they expect you to stop by and greet them. It felt like I've never left the job. Initially, I felt obligated to concern myself with the plight of my clients when I saw their faces even while off the clock. After a while, I would choose to drive an extra distance to go around certain houses and avoid being seen.

On the bus shuttle, I saw a prior client with legal involvement that attempted to disregard the program's expectations for successful completion and was disrespectful towards me. We just exchanged looks, and I continued to read my book. There was a great amount of countertransference. Just being in his presence altered my mood and not in a positive way. Also, I saw a prior client that committed various violent crimes in Walmart. There were definitely clients that I counseled in that boot camp I never wanted to see again, especially in public.

Moreover, I saw another young client that I met in the inpatient psychiatric unit at the post office. He had the audacity to insult me because of my clothing and shoes. I did not wear the most expensive name brands but I dressed comfortably and diplomatic. At work, I may have ignored that comment and attempted to analyze why he felt the need to build himself up by trying to tear me down. However, off the clock I was not about to invest my time to explore his underlying thoughts; I had just enough time to assert how my appearance should not be a concern of his and walked off with pride.

Further, I went to Publix and walked pass this prior female client that I initially met as an intern in a community mental health center. She rolled her eyes at me with an attitude. She stated she was not expecting to see me outside of the treatment setting. I was thinking that the feeling was mutual as I nodded my head and kept moving.

The experiences that really made me feel uncomfortable occurred when clients knew where I lived or were in close proximity to it. I was driving toward my apartment one day about to pull in until I saw a prior client that was in a substance abuse treatment program walking pass my entrance. I hurriedly pulled down the sun visor in my car to avoid him noticing me and decided to pull in at a different entrance.

Another incident that made me feel very uncomfortable was when one of the youth juvenile offenders said he saw me pulling into my parents' home. Sometimes they're watching you when you're not even aware of it. It's quite unnerving for folks to know where you stay. However, it's even more unsettling when you know about the vicious crimes some clients committed, and they now know where people you love reside.

Overall, there were times that I felt trapped and didn't want to interface within the community due to fear of being seen by clients, especially the ones that were intertwined with the criminal justice system. I didn't want to go out and enjoy myself. I became extra vigilant of my surroundings after hearing so many horror stories. I placed myself in a box captive by my own self-imposed fear of being stalked and harassed by clients. However, the truly violent and mentally unstable clients never crossed paths with me outside of the therapeutic setting, thank God. As a result, I began to release my fear and came to the realization that even if we crossed paths, I've done my best to uplift humanity and any further chance encounter will result in a positive experience. The latter experiences were positive and clients were smiling and happy to report on the progress they've made with their lives.

Working in residential programs for kids

For the providers in residential adolescent programs, you really need to have an inner motivation to work in that environment for the amount of financial compensation. With a degree in psychology, as a resident manager I earned only $9.00 an hour. It becomes tolerable to work in an environment where you deal with bad attitudes, and your paycheck reflects how valued you are as an employee. But when your paycheck forces you to live with relatives to help you out, that's a problem. It was for me! I came to work stressed, annoyed, and looking for a way out. I worked there for a month and thankfully found a full time job as a prevention specialist/case manager earning $13.00 an hour. I worked the full time position but still worked as the resident manager as needed when I wanted some extra money. Working for the $9.00 was an option, not a necessity to maintain my livelihood; that's a big difference.

I've had two incidents that confirmed that working in an adolescent program as a career choice long term was not for me. While at a juvenile offender level 6 residential program, this one juvenile cursed me out because he didn't advance to the next level; he had refused to complete an individual counseling session with me. He would attend group but refused to meet with me one on one. I should have advocated for him to advance because clients should have the option to refuse an individual session if they won't benefit from it. But being within my 3 months probationary period, I said nothing and suffered the consequence.

However, the most traumatic experience was working at the residential adolescent residential program. This one teen cursed me out with derogatory terms that I had not healed from during my childhood. His words cut me deep and almost put me to tears. My eyes were beginning to water, and my co-worker/best friend stood up for me. She told him to discontinue his verbal assault on me while we were outside under the gazebo. The hardest part about that experience was that I had to take in all that negative criticism but unable to criticize him back. Too wrongs may not make it right but it can be soothing to a broken spirit. It's not a good feeling when someone can say awful things to you and you can't defend yourself. They say during orientation trainings, don't take it personal; however, some comments from clients are personal attacks. One can't help but to take it personal! You have to internalize those negative comments until your shift is over. Hopefully as soon as you're off the job, you'll finally be able to release it. Thank goodness I had my friend there who helped me through the mental anguish I felt in that moment.

Overall, I would advise you to make sure you work with a population that's best suited for helping you nurture your wounds, not make them deeper. My adolescent years were quite tumultuous for me and working around teens caused certain memories that were buried to resurface. Working with adolescents at the residential level 6 boot camp, those officers rarely tolerated any disrespect. However, if you're in a work place setting where it's only you and one other co-worker with 12 or more unruly teens, it can be mentally draining. You're there to encourage and motivate others but not at your own expense.

Sometimes jobs can be scarce, and we have to get what we can get until we do better. I still encourage you to keep looking. There is another job out there where you can work full time. If you have the tolerance and have worked through your own trauma, you can still work in a residential program as needed or part-time.

Know what's not for you

Sometimes you have to work with issues of target populations that are of no interest to you. Honestly, I detest marriage/couples counseling. After each session as social worker in the inpatient behavioral health unit, I felt even more annoyed. I'm grateful that I only had to facilitate three couple sessions during my entire career in this field. I listened attentively and offered textbook solutions but my heart wasn't fully committed to resolving the unhealthy dynamics of their relationships.

I was happily single and being matchmaker for individuals was not a role I preferred to take on. I had my own love life to manage. I knew after the third session that the only marriage or couples counseling done in my presence would be during treatment team meeting with other clinical providers present. I would allow the treatment team members to attempt to solve long standing relationship issues in five minutes. I would refer them to an outpatient therapist that specialized in relationship counseling. I had no problem admitting when I couldn't help someone and sent them to someone who could.

It can also be frustrating when you've provided therapy and great discharge planning for a patient, and that patient is readmitted inpatient within a week reporting the same presenting problem. Sometimes patients would be discharged from inpatient that morning and show back up in the emergency room that night. Some patients would sell their medications and report feeling suicidal to receive more prescriptions. After a while, I loss complete motivation for facilitating psychotherapy groups because I was discussing the same topics with the same patients. As a result, I decided to switch from working the unit as the social worker to working as intake specialist. It is okay to be honest with yourself. Always assess your strengths, weaknesses, likes, and dislikes on a continual basis.

Staying balanced: Sleep

It is extremely important to nourish your mind, body, and spirit. There have been times when I didn't, and the life energy that used sustain me departed leaving me utterly exhausted. Throughout the day, I felt so drained and was suffocating in a sea of peoples' problems. Every breath I took was reserved for me, and I didn't have the strength to breathe life into someone else that was reaching out to me for hope and inspiration.

It was very difficult to receive an adequate amount of sleep during the work week. I would usually have to recuperate and catch up on sleep on my days off. It was difficult for me to educate patients on the importance of sleep when I was getting 3-4 hours of sleep each night. Sometimes, it would take a few hours for me to release all of the traumatic and problematic issues that were haunting others from my own mind. During some nights, I was unable to sleep throughout the night because I was reliving other people's trauma and revisiting them in a dream as if I was the victim. I had great attending and listening skills which we were taught to have in school and on the job training. Unfortunately, I was too in tune with the patients' experience and unable to detach myself from it.

Exercise was a lifeline for me. It was not an option, but a requirement during each week. The only times I found it difficult to exercise was when my calves swelled causing me pain because of my history of blood clots from deep vein thrombosis. Sometimes, I had to make a difficult choice between my mind unraveling to the point of a mental breakdown or my physical health.

Staying balanced: TV, Reading & Vacation

I had to be mindful of what television shows to watch and which ones to avoid. Certain reality intervention shows where families confronted others about mental illness or substance abuse were avoided at all cost. I kept that television remote in hand to quickly change the channel when a commercial advertising psychotropic medications, mental illness, or substance abuse treatment appeared on screen. I had no desire to hear about or see reality television shows where fighting and arguments dominated the entire show; the intention was to simply entertain the viewers, not help the participants. I already witnessed too much conflict on the job with employees and clients and needed a break from all of that turmoil during my time off.

However, there were some scripted TV series and documentaries that I truly enjoyed that was entertaining and informative such as delightful reruns of *Golden Girls, 227, Martin, and Will & Grace.* My favorite television series is Tyler Perry's *The Have and Have Nots*. I would also receive great insight and inspiration from Oprah Winfrey's *Lifeclass, Master class, and Super Soul Sunday* on the Oprah Winfrey Network. The authors and motivational speakers featured on her shows gave me encouragement which I desperately needed. I also read the inspirational books of featured guests of the Oprah Winfrey show as well as fiction novels that were simply entertaining. I would enjoy sitting on my patio reading, meditating, and listening to inspirational gospel music which healed my mind. As a clinician, it's easy to find others that you can uplift but places to find your own source of inspiration are few. Further, I would also travel home to visit family, and I always felt renewed every time I left.

It's also important to take a vacation and travel outside of your immediate area for a change of scenery to refresh your soul. I decided to travel to Miami to attend Oprah's Live the Life You Want weekend tour in 2014, and it was spectacular. The positivity and energy in the arena was magnificent. Inspirational Oprah Winfrey spoke to me afterwards and stated "I saw you down there". Thus, even when you feel less than at times or overlooked on the job, God sees your importance and will utilize others to remind you of your tremendous value in this world. Overall, you have to take a leap of faith and surround yourself with people that motivate you and immerse yourself in positive environments that nurture your self-esteem and well-being.

Staying balanced: Fix it or leave it alone

It's okay to decline helping everyone. It wasn't healthy for me and downright impossible to fix every problem that was brought to my attention. When you find yourself trying to save the world, meditate and reflect immediately. If your soul is stirring you to help, then do it. But if it's just an impulse that quickly dissipates and an uneasy feeling surfaces, then don't.

Sometimes working in the helping profession, we carry a look that we care. Strangers would approach me asking for money or request that I drive them to their destination. Mere acquaintacies or classmates would feel comfortable enough asking for favors even though we weren't even friends. I would politely decline offering assistance and not feel guilty about it after a few times of practicing saying no. However, I will never forget when a 12 year old boy in his school uniform came up to me and asked for money so he and his mother can stay in the motel for the night. I said I didn't have any cash on me which I didn't at the time. I saw his mom standing under the tree. I thought to myself "all of these people in the parking lot but yet they've singled me out and asked me". As I pulled off, and dropped off some books to the library, my heart was moved. I told myself I would stop by the bank and withdraw $40 and return back to that Walmart. If they were still there, I would assist them; if not, I would continue with my day. I came back, and they were still there. As soon as I handed them the cash, they said thank you and left the area. I felt good but not overwhelmed. It’s always wise to use discernment when extending acts of kindness especially if that good deed will be at the expense of your personal finances and time.

Staying balanced: Eat properly and use the restroom

While working at the hospital performing intake, I would be on call and that cell phone would continue to ring. As soon as I began to eat, the phone rang with the emergency room staff wanting me to come downstairs immediately to assess a patient. Oftentimes, I would binge eat because I didn't know when I would have time to eat a snack. Sometimes I would walk around very hungry nearly about to pass out. Some days were extremely busy, and I wasn't even able to urinate in peace. I would develop the unhealthy habit of holding my urine, and sometimes it felt as though I was urinating inside of myself. I could feel the urine flowing in my stomach. I began to have stomach problems with no other explanation other than stress. I ended up seeing a gastroenterologist, and he didn't know what to do. The medication he prescribed didn't help at all, and I nearly choked on it. I discontinued that medication after a week and came to the realization that I need to change the way I respond to other's demands. I decided to set boundaries and tell physicians to give me about 10-15 minutes. Other times I allowed the call go to voicemail and returned the call later. Further, I began to take a full lunch break like everyone else was instead of ending mine early. My mind and body felt much better after those progressive changes in how I responded to constant pressure and demands.

Respect my time off

Oftentimes your co-workers and supervisor pay no regards to your personal time when you're off the clock. I've never been on call at any jobs but my director and co-workers still felt comfortable enough to contact me on my personal cell phone. Anytime I would see that hospital number flashing across my phone, I did not answer. Later, my director would text me constantly or put me in a group text. Being reminded of the occurrences on the job when you're off is stressful. It's like you've never left.

One incident that angered me was when my co-worker sent me at text message at 7:15 in the morning asking me to work for her in two weeks so she can attend a music concert. To make matters worse, she was going to see me later that day during shift report since I came to relieve her. Thus, that request could have waited. I texted her back later that afternoon stating "don't ever text my cell phone again this early in the morning. I'm not on call". Furthermore, I verbalized my discontent with her thinking she had the right to contact me at her convenience but not mine. She was at work but I wasn't.

Sometimes the unit secretary would call me to see if I wanted to work since somebody called out. I never answered and sent the unit secretary to voicemail. I decided against reporting to work at the last minute due to someone calling out. I truly needed time off to reflect on my week and evaluate my decisions. I've realized that there will be more opportunities to earn more income but my time is of more value than any dollar amount that job could offer. I didn't care if they requested for me to just work 1 or 2 hours. Walking into a stressful workplace environment can negatively impact you for the rest of the day, especially when the energy is hostile. It's just not worth it!

Oftentimes, my shift would be ending in 5 or 10 minutes and a physician would walk in requesting I evaluate a patient. However, when you evaluate a patient which could take 30 minutes to an hour, you also must document the encounter. There had been times when I worked 14-15 hour days due to me trying to accommodate others. I realized that everyone else leaves on time during shift change so why am I overextending myself as if my time for me is less precious than their time to them. It's okay to respectfully decline another task. Take care of yourself because oftentimes you'll only be valued by what you do but not necessarily who you are.

Stress kills

This line of work can be the death of you if you allow it. Even though management in behavioral health professions may have counseling degrees, they may not be the least bit concerned about overwhelming you with work that jeopardizes your physical, mental, and emotional health. It amazes me how so empathetic they appear to be with clients but some supervisors demonstrate lack of concern for your well-being. While serving as a prevention specialist, I had to manage nearly 70 cases of juvenile offenders that was previously shared by four counselors before my arrival. I'm glad that program loss funding and closed down approaching my 5th month of employment there. Thankfully, the agency I worked for was large enough and I was able to be placed in another county as a case manager.

One of the most challenging and stressful patients for me to handle were those diagnosed with developmental disabilities. They kept coming back to the emergency room because they didn't want to stay in their group home. They are initially pleasant in the hospital but when it's time to be discharged, their behavior changed. Some began beating their heads against the wall, cursing, hitting, and throwing feces on the wall. It takes so much energy to deescalate them. I have the upmost respect for workers serving that specific population.

It can be a very hostile work environment at times in the emergency room. Patients became more irritated because they've been waiting for hours with nothing to eat or drink. Oftentimes, the reason there is nothing to eat is because the employees chose not to bring their own lunch and ate the food designated for the patients. Secondly, as I worked overnight, management wanted patients discharged as soon as possible so they can continue to advertise short ER wait times on billboards. However, half of those patients walking in overnight had no one to pick them up, couldn't return home, or were homeless. Management would just say give them a bus pass and discharge them to a shelter. However, city buses aren't running at 2:00am, and it cost to live at a shelter. The first day at a shelter may be free. However, if that individual already used up their free days for the year, it would cost them $10/day.

In addition, while serving as an outpatient counselor for substance abuse treatment, I managed nearly 65 clients for months. I had the most clients amongst the counselors in the entire agency but yet some counselors had only 3 or 4 clients. The associations/organizations that monitored this agency mandated that no counselor shall have a caseload of over 50 at any given time. However, these agencies rarely get accurately audited for compliance with regulations.

As an outpatient counselor, I had clients referred from so many different places such as, DUI programs, drug court, family dependency court, child protective investigations, prison diversion, department of corrections, employee assistance programs and other agencies. I had to submit legal reports, perform group and individual counseling, and ensure fee collections from all these patients. During this time period, I felt stress in my body for the first time in my life and was about to lose my breath one evening. I walked out of the building to relax my mind and body.

During audit time, I would see how stressed out my co-worker was who worked in quality improvement. This female co-worker was responsible for ensuring medical chart compliance. Consequently, she died in her office while preparing for the audit. She was found bent over on her desk due to a heart attack. She was dead before the ambulance arrived. Another co-worker at the same agency had medical issues which worsened because of the stress on the job. He ended up passing away shortly thereafter she did. Those deaths sent chills up my spine when I walked down those hallways. I knew I had to make a departure soon. I didn’t know where at the time, but I knew I had to go.

At my next job on the medical and psychiatric unit, my stress level skyrocketed. I was hired as the licensed clinical social worker for a brand new behavioral health unit in a hospital that had no experience in operating one. The patients, staff, and corporate had me on the brink of losing my mind that first year. Now, there are three full time staff clinicians, student interns, and two part time staff members performing the tasks that were assigned to me alone for nearly a full year. I was performing all the assessments, therapy groups, facilitating treatment teams, and discharges each week in a very hostile environment. When I think of the trials and tribulations I had to overcome, it was nobody but God that helped me maintain my sanity.

Unfortunately, the unit coordinator on the behavioral health unit that was hired along with me ended up committing suicide two years later after opening the unit. I saw her one morning at work looking stressed out. She said to the nursing manager that she knew she was late and probably would be written up. She appeared so defeated. Consequently, she shot herself that night. In addition, a young newly hired psychiatrist that worked on our unit became a patient at another behavioral health unit and consequently killed himself. Further, one of our therapists committed suicide after relapsing on illicit drugs as his life was spiraling out of control. I pray that if I ever got to that point of planning to commit suicide, I'm able to reach out for help and actually receive it. Sometimes we call out for help but no one is truly listening or paying attention to behavioral cues because we're the ones designated to provide the care, not be the recipient of it.

Toxic friends and co-workers

Another tool I utilized to stay balanced was to avoid certain associates that would only call and text to dump their issues onto me. They never called me to see how I was doing. Once I came to that awareness, I stopped picking up the phone or responding especially after I brought it to their attention, and they still didn't change. Also, I choose not to engage in lengthy dialogue via text messaging. Enough is enough. I felt if someone was genuinely concerned about my well-being, they would pick up the phone and call.

By all means, I would avoid eating lunch with co-workers. The one or two times I did, the conversation consisted of complaints about the job. I don't need that negativity during my lunch break. If they weren't complaining about the job, they would be trying to ask about my personal life which was a topic I was not about to elaborate on. The majority of my coworkers demonstrated that they could not be trusted with personal business which could be used to hinder your growth within a company. I would go to the roof of the parking garage or find an office to eat in peaceful solitude.

Difficult conversations

One of most challenging aspects of this job is having a heart to heart with patients that no one had been successful doing. As long as you are genuine and have good intentions with the advice you give, most of the patients readily receive it. One male client in the outpatient program had an odor that could be smelled down the hall. It was really bad and it lingered. I could tell he was quite depressed and was just in outpatient treatment because he had an open case with child protective investigations for possible neglect. The child protective investigator told me that he had an odor, and the wife knew it but no one addressed it with him. We had to staff his case because he missed a group counseling session. A staff member who I've seen confront chronic substance abusers or criminal offenders didn't even have the courage to say something to that patient. He just told me "let's make this as quickly as possible cause of that stench".

I asked the patient to see me the next day for individual counseling. Honestly, I was nervous because I've never had to address this type of issue with any of my clients in the past. I brought his hygiene to his attention in a sensitive manner and spoke out of true concern because I noticed how people would frown and criticize him. He was depressed, and we addressed his low self-esteem. I could relate with having low self-esteem and depression, and someone took time to empower me resulting in me having a more positive self-image of myself.

The following week his hygiene was so much better. He was able to get a job at a fast food restaurant and walked with his head up as he attended group. He participated more and no longer sat against the wall with his head down. Overall, sometimes we have to do what's best for the client, not always what's easiest for us. It would have been easier for me to ignore that problem and just address the substance abuse issue. However, if you notice another problem that's worth addressing, then do it. From my experience, the clients readily received the feedback and expressed appreciation for it.

Sexual advances from patients

If you work in this field, you are bound to have patients that may flirt with you. Some of the female counselors and nurses would have their breasts grabbed by male patients who claimed to be psychotic but yet weren't grabbing the chest of male staff members. It was interesting how some patients could exhibit symptoms of psychosis at his/her convenience. Also, one female patient told me "I find you very attractive" and tried to rub my chest. Another female patient stated "I love your physique, it's a pleasure to look at you". One male patient that was arguing and attempting to fight other patients tried to grope me in his room. As I entered, he tried to close the door behind me and kept trying to touch my buttocks. Another male client in the emergency room kept trying to hold my hand, wink his eyes and inquire about my sexual preference. I would remind those patients with loose boundaries that their comments or sexual advances were inappropriate and unacceptable. When you set boundaries, be firm and assertive. No need to be aggressive but definitely not passive either.

People calling for information

I would remind providers to make sure a written consent is in the chart before you disclose information about a patient's clinical information. Sometime, patients give verbal consent for family or friend collateral but make sure you document it thoroughly. Also, look at the caller ID of the caller to see if it matches up with the phone number of the family member listed in the patient's medical record.

In particular, this one mother was continuously changing her mind about wanting her son to discharge home with her after his inpatient stay on the behavioral health unit. While at the nursing station, the patient's sister called pretending to be the mother. The sister stated the patient can't come back home because of a court order. Ironically, the unit coordinator was on the phone with the sister pretending to be the mother; I was sitting next to the unit coordinator speaking with the actual mother. The patient never signed a consent for his sister. I told the unit coordinator to hang up the phone because that was not the mother. Hence, it is okay to place callers on hold while you review the chart. That approach is more preferable than having patients attempting to sue you after their discharge because of a breach in confidentiality even if it was by accident.

Walking into a lion's den

While I worked as a children's case manager, I had to visit many clients in their homes. There will be times when you walk into a home and not know what to do to bring about peace. All of that textbook knowledge was helpful when working in a controlled work office environment. However, when you walk into the fire ignited by family conflict escalating out of control, you have to adapt to your surroundings and use common sense.

In particular, this adolescent client was cursing back and forth with his mother with several relatives in the house. That family feud was getting out of control. I called the therapist that was supposed to be assisting me and told him to come over right away. As soon as he arrived, I left. I had kept the peace and now it was up to that therapist to maintain it.

When doing home visits, make sure you take someone else with you if possible and work as a team depending on the neighborhood. One therapist and I would always meet up at a home together if the client's insurance paid for both a therapist and case manager. However, there was one client in particular whose insurance only paid for him to have a case manager. I was aware that this particular apartment complex consisted of street gang members, violence, and drugs. I followed my instinct and decided to visit the family before that sun went down. I brought a Bible because the client's mom requested one.

As I was walking pass one building, I saw a teenager come around the corner, then go back. As I continued to walk in that direction, I saw another teenager peek around the corner. I could sense that something was wrong, and I didn't feel safe. As soon as I turned that corner, there were about 9-10 guys about to attack or rob me, but a few of them saw the Bible in my hand. They looked at me, and their demeanor changed. I spoke and kept walking. I'm grateful that I visited that client during daylight. If I had arrived in the late evening, they may not have seen the type of book I was holding. The outcome of my visit could have been disastrous for me.

My advice is that if you can't visit certain patients in the early afternoon, visit them first thing in the morning. Night time visits should be reserved for areas that don't have a reported history of violence and crime. Your life is of more value than productivity as measured by some agency. If something were to happen to you because you decided to take unnecessary risk, that agency would not support you. You have to look out for yourself.

Even in a secure locked behavioral health unit, you need to be careful because the patients' behaviors can be quite unpredictable and violent. I remember I knocked on a female patient's door to complete an assessment, and she jumped out of her bed and began threatening bodily harm to me with her fist balled up coming at me. She had contagious illnesses, and I did not want to be hit by her. I did not turn my back but slowly walked backwards and exited the room. She slammed the door afterwards. The hospital management and corporate may not be satisfied that certain questions weren't answered in the assessment; I would simply reply that the patient was unable to fully assessed at this time. Administration is sitting behind his/her computer screens looking at data but not risking being physically hurt. A simple interview is not worth compromising your safety.

Oftentimes, working in the psychiatric emergency room that holds patients who are actively suicidal, homicidal or highly intoxicated with alcohol or drugs can be quite dangerous. Patients would occasionally come in during my shift with knives, guns, needles with fluids oftentimes due to the nurse or technician overlooking the tasks of taking inventory of their belongings or using a wand to detect metal objects upon initial entry. Also, even though monitor technicians' are sitting in front of the cameras, some are actually watching movies on their cell phones or looking at cars or houses on the computer. As a result, you have to be your best surveillance system. You must carefully assess the patients' behaviors, items in that room, and the behaviors of your coworkers. If patients feel they have nothing else to live for, and at their wits end, be on guard. Also, it's important to distinguish acts of self-harm that are cries for help or attention from their significant others versus self-harm attempts due to not caring if they live or die. At those moments, they could care less about themselves or me for that matter. It’s good to have supportive staff to intervene when necessary but even better to create a peaceful atmosphere where you set the tone for the interactions with potentially hostile patients. You really don’t know what type of weapon a patient may have so carefully chose your words, be mindful of your body language, and bring an overwhelming amount of positive energy into that room. You can instill hope into the heart of someone feeling hopeless and maintain a safe work environment.

Unfortunately, some patients are just violent with antisocial personality disorders and no amount of medications or therapy will change their attitude. One young male patient punched a nurse and broke his nose; he later punched the recreational therapist and broke his nose. He attempted to fight a staff member every opportunity given. Another patient that had an extensive criminal history grabbed the scissors from the medication nurse and stabbed another patient. A female patient in the emergency room hit the female nurse and bragged about hitting her to law enforcement. Thus, every patient admitted on a behavioral health unit doesn’t necessarily have a mental illness but will have a diagnosis for insurance purposes. Before interacting with patients with violent tendencies, look over their chart, gather information from other staff members, pay close attention to their behavior, and invite another staff member with you for the interview. Your safety is important; you can’t help everyone so help where you can and leave the rest to God.

This supervisor needs supervision

The problem with developing close knit relationships with the supervisor is that I would be given additional work to complete. Plus, supervisors would complain about their bosses to me but I couldn't complain about them. Those conversations were not balanced; it's draining when you've become a sounding board for their frustrations.

Oftentimes in the mental health field, men are in director/management positions even though it appears to be a female dominated profession. There always seems to be a male in a superior position which is unfair. On the other hand, one female director removed me from my private office into an office space shared with four women while she moved one of those females into my office. That female co-worker and I just switched places, and we were on the same level. Do you think a female would have been moved into an office space with men, and a male put into her office without eyebrows being raised? Unfortunately, gender discrimination does occur but oftentimes overlooked when the injured party is male.

Some supervisors abuse their power and are very inconsiderate. While working as an outpatient counselor, I had put in for vacation time and was approved for nearly 2 months. It was the Thursday before my vacation; my male supervisor wanted to take a vacation during my week off so he denied me two days before the start of my paid time off. He took off that week saying he forgot I had that time off. I had to take the following week off after he returned from his vacation.

This same outpatient supervisor told me not to report for court even though I received a court subpoena and phone call from the state attorney. He didn't want to manage my caseload for a few hours. He said the agency will handle it if a failure to appear warrant was issued. I was not about to put my freedom in the hands of a supervisor I didn't trust or in an agency that appeared more concerned about money than people. I emailed him and the vice president stating I didn't feel comfortable ignoring a subpoena. He and I had an argument in the hallway the day before because he forbid me to attend court. I showed up for court which didn't even take up much time. I was able to return to work that morning and still complete my work related tasks. You have to stand up for yourself and always abide by the judicial system. The most your job can do is fire you but a judge can incarcerate you.

Employee evaluation should be renamed employer retaliation. Working at the hospital, the employees would be given a survey in May to discuss how satisfied we were with our place of employment. If you have problematic issues you want to address, that's the time to do it. I made sure I used that opportunity to shed light to corporate about the unethical events occurring on the behavioral health unit. However, once that director receives feedback about how dissatisfied I was, my employer used my evaluation in June to retaliate against me. Most people in directors or people in leadership positions in healthcare are so accustomed to giving constructive criticism to their subordinates but don't receive negative feedback about their leadership skills very well.

One of the nursing managers revealed to me that the new director confided in her about how hospital management and corporate leaders advised her to watch out for me. However, in light of the hostility directed towards me from management and corporate, I surpassed the expectations for my job positions while being highly favored by patients. A supervisor or director can scheme day and night to terminate you from a job. However, as long as you carry out your tasks and become indispensable, they really have no legal justification to terminate you. You can contest and successfully overcome underhanded political maneuvers to force you out. I have been called into human resources several times but my quality of work spoke for itself.

I would advise you to always put your concerns in an email so you'll have written documentation. One director kept emphasizing that I come and talk to her about my concerns because e-mails are discoverable. However, I didn't trust her and strongly believe that important matters must be communicated via email. Oftentimes, managers will lie and downright deny that a conversation ever took place. You have to protect yourself and document everything. I documented the approximate date and time incidents and conversations occurred, especially when I expressed concerns about unethical and illegal practices.

PART II: KNOWLEDGE FOR PATIENTS, COURTS, GENERAL PUBLIC

Residential Adolescent programs-for parents

Before you send your kids that are having problems with drugs to a treatment program, it may be helpful to be aware of some of the consequences of that decision. Human resources aren't always the most thorough in their background/reference checks of employees that will be supervising your children. In particular, this co-ed residential program I worked at hired a female staff member that revealed she was recently terminated at her previous place of employment for engaging in sexual relations with male teens at another group home. She ended up attempting to sleep with one of the male teens in the residential program we worked at.

At the same residential program, the residential supervisor that hired me was great. However, he was promoted to a higher level position and replaced by another male supervisor. Unfortunately, the new supervisor didn't do a great job of staffing and several times there weren't any female staff members that worked overnight. That new residential supervisor volunteered to work overnight while a female co-worker worked; he decided to walk down the female bedrooms and elicit sex from a 15 year old female. This girl reported it to her mom and the therapist, and he ended up being terminated.

Further, I had a close friend of mine with a criminal justice degree and no adult criminal record. He wanted to attain employment using his degree. I mentioned to him about a job opening at a substance abuse center for adults and adolescents. He applied and used me as a reference. Human resources called me and left a message; I called them back urging them to call me so I could give feedback. However, the call was never returned. I felt he would be a good fit only with adult men in an outpatient or residential program.

However, he was placed as a counselor in a co-ed male and female adolescent residential program. A few months later, I saw his picture in a local paper being accused of sexual relations with one of the adolescent female clients in the program; he was convicted and sentenced to several years in prison. Thus, I would just encourage agencies to make sure there is follow up with these references because the input they give is valuable.

Overall, parents or relatives make sure you inquire from treatment centers about any incidents where adolescent patients were harmed by staff or other clients. They may not be disclose everything but at least you’ve done all that you can do to protect your loved one. Your inquisitive nature will cause them to be extra cautious with how they treat your loved one especially if you are familiar with the governing entities that audit that program, such as Department of Children and Families.

Escaping legal persecution

There appears to be a growing trend among people that have pending criminal charges. Many clients would check themselves into the emergency room voluntarily for suicidal thoughts or psychosis. However, they would be banging on the social work office door the next morning demanding that a fax be sent to the courthouse with their admission paperwork with the hope of being excused from court. Staff members would remark how come the auditory hallucinations or depressive thoughts expressed initially dissipated so quickly.

Many offenders that violated probation or missed a court appearance were prompted by their attorney to check themselves into an inpatient behavioral health program. Some patients committed crimes over and over again. They would go to jail for one day and then be released to a mental health agency. That mental health agency would release them within a few hours sometimes.

I was so astonished by the honesty of this one female patient who admitted she got drunk and ran into a tree. She said "word on the street" told her that if she ever gets into legal trouble, she should tell the officer that the voices told her to do it. She said she preferred to be in a hospital for a day or two than going to jail and dealing with court costs and DUI programs.

One male patient was arrested at Walmart for shoplifting. During the arrest, he said he was delusional and having a heart attack. As soon as he arrived in the ER at the hospital and after the police left, he checked himself out of the hospital. On a different note, a female patient robbed and assaulted someone the previous day and took an overdose the following day. Remarkably, patients sometimes will admit that the medication taken wasn't enough to actually harm them but just enough to get them admitted to the behavioral health unit.

Some patients had arrest warrants and tried to hide out in the hospital. Several patients refused to sign consent for their probation officer. Other patients would sign a release and request that only their admission but not their urine drug screens or discharge date. However, once a release of information is signed for the department of corrections, they can access all the records but most often just inquire about when the patient is being discharged. As a healthcare professional, it's very important to communicate with the department of corrections so you're not perceived as partially responsible for a patient's criminal actions once they've departed.

Secondary Gain

As soon as some of those patients walked on the unit, they were requesting to speak with me to complete their paperwork for disability. I respectfully declined, and stated your primary psychiatrist or physician who has been providing care for you should be completing these forms. I've only worked with them for 2-3 hours, and oftentimes their hospital stay was no longer than 3 days. From what patients reported, it's easier for them to be approved for social security benefits with a mental illness diagnosis than medical diagnosis.

One male patient during his assessment stated he hasn't been inpatient in years but was up for review with social security. He stated he had to be hospitalized in order keep receiving his benefits. He stated he wasn't really depressed but losing his income would make him depressed.

This one female patient stated she told her father she overdosed on medication so he would feel guilty and pay her mortgage. She laughed about it during group therapy. In addition, some patients are continuously checking themselves in to find romantic dates with the other patients. I saw patients exchanging phone numbers quite frequently. Some patients were caught having sex on camera on the unit.

Several patients came in stating they just needed some food and a place to stay, especially towards the end of the month. They stated they spent their money and their social security check wouldn't come until the first or third. Approaching the end of the month, the behavioral health unit would be full of patients but during the first and third, the census would decline. As soon their check was deposited, some stated they wanted to be discharged and admitted to reporting feeling suicidal but didn't truly mean it.

However, no matter what the ulterior motive a patient seeks treatment, its best to look past that and give your best to help them meet their needs. Coming to work with a positive approach for the work you do will help you get through the day. Oftentimes, people come for one thing, and leave with something of greater value. A kind word, understanding glance, and imparting a sense of feeling valued are things that may appear trivial but can make a world of difference in someone's life.

Violation of patient rights

It is very important for patients and families to know the basic right of clients in mental health inpatient facilities. It is equally important to know the laws that these facilities are supposed to adhere to when providing care. People that are not fully aware of their rights will continue to have their rights trampled on.

In particular, this elderly female patient was held involuntary under the Baker Act and was approaching a length of inpatient stay for nearly 30 days. She had straight Medicare so the psychiatrist continued to ask for continuances with the court. If that patient had no insurance or a managed HMO that cut off payments to the hospital, that patient would have been discharged earlier.

At her morning court hearing, the magistrate ordered that she be released immediately from the hospital because she did not meet criteria to be held there against her will. The magistrate ordered for her to be released before midnight. As the afternoon approached and I was about to get off work, I noticed that the nurse and doctor appeared nonchalant about discharging her off the unit. As a result, I sent an email to the director of ethics, risk management, directors, case management advising them that holding this patient after she was court ordered to be released is false imprisonment.

I reported to work the next morning, and the patient was still on the unit. My email was acknowledged but no one in authoritative positions responded. My director informed the staff members to not make the patient upset during her prolonged stay on the unit. On that day, I refused to participate in any treatment activities with that patient knowing she was being held illegally. She was released that day after I continued verbalize my concerns of false imprisonment.

Also, some patients that walked into the emergency room requesting voluntary admission ended up as an involuntary admission solely due to insurance companies authorizing more days for an involuntary admission versus a voluntary one. As a result, healthcare professionals were pressured by management to initiate an involuntary hold on patients even though it was documented that they voluntarily sought help for the deterioration in their mental health.

On a different note, one female patient was placed in four point restraints for several hours and no vital signs were documented for nearly 6 hours. This patient could have experienced compromised skin integrity, elevated heart rate and blood pressure. Further, the overnight staff attempted to straight cauterize her and get a urine sample but was unsuccessful. This female patient experienced previous trauma so now one could only imagine how traumatic it was to be pinned down while a male staff member is inserting an object into her vagina. Furthermore, it wasn’t even documented that staff attempted to cauterize her; I inquired that following morning because urine was all over the floor in her room. Thus, it is so important for family members and friends to be present during the arrival of their loved ones in behavioral healthcare settings, especially the emergency room. Staff respond noticeable different when a patient is alone versus when a patient is accompanied with caring friends and relatives watching everything. Patients are more vulnerable to being unintentionally mistreated if they are alone.

Some emergency room physicians would initiate a legal hold for mental health purposes with the underlying intention to punish the patient. One ER physician even boasted about it when a male patient challenged that physician's medical knowledge. Further, there has been a recent trend of elderly patients being held against their will under mental health law when they desire to sign themselves out of the hospital against medical advice. Their competency is continuously questioned; sometimes it's warranted but most of the times, it's not. However, the elderly is a very vulnerable population and oftentimes are not given a choice in regards to making their own medical decisions. Certain medical providers with authority fail to realize that holding a person who doesn't meet medical necessity against their will in the hospital can be traumatizing.

Transfer or accept

Working as the intake specialist in the emergency room, I was instructed by management and a corporate entity to encourage patients presenting with psychiatric issues that had no insurance to transfer out to a community based facility. Uninsured patients were basically undesirable admissions. I was also pressured by the emergency department to get them out as soon as possible. However, I was very familiar with the federal Emtala law in place to prevent hospitals from transferring patients out solely based on insurance. Certain laws protected the patient's right to be given treatment at the hospital of their choice.

When making a decision to transfer or accept on the unit, I would take into consideration how close the patient's support system was in proximity to the hospital. Also, I would determine if the risks outweighed the benefit of the transfer. I didn't want the patient being billed unnecessarily from the hospital either especially if they could be placed in a funded community health center and not pay for treatment. Most patients were already tired and exhausted after being transported by the police or emergency medical services so most were not in agreement to be transported again. Most importantly, if the patient didn't sign written consent to be transferred out, I did not transfer them out in light of being constantly harassed by ER staff or corporate management. I stood firm on the principle of doing right by patients. Unfortunately, most of my coworkers and the transfer center transferred them out without their written consent.

Further, patients without insurance had to wait in the psychiatric emergency room for at least 12 hours according to management while patients with insurances were admitted right away after being medically cleared. Discrimination against the poor at its finest. On one occasion, I recommended an unfunded patient that has been waiting for several hours to be admitted to the behavioral health unit after witnessing a deterioration in their mental health due to their psychiatric needs not being met in the emergency room. However, a funded patient was just brought into the emergency room and the transfer center wanted that funded patient that was waiting for a few minutes to take precedence over an unfunded patient that had been waiting for over 6 hours. I decided against it and advocated for the unfunded patient, and consequently, a complaint was filed against me to the corporate vice president.

If the patient was in an incapacitated state either from being psychotic, very sedated from an overdose in a suicide attempt, I refused to transfer them out without a health care proxy or advocate. I was very clear and assertive about treating all patient's equally and fairly and dealt with the verbal reprimands from management later.

Overall, if you are uninsured, follow up to make sure a written consent to be transferred out was even signed. If not, your rights may have been violated. Unless patients or families speak up about it, it will continue to happen. Some patients were transferred unnecessarily counties away and had to pay for their own transportation back home. Management told employees to just explain the financial benefits of transferring but not describe the therapeutic environment of the facility they were being sent. I was an intern at the only two community based mental health centers in the county so I would give them accurate perspectives of what they could expect to experience. The only pain medications they would normally receive were over the counter. At one community mental health center, patients just sat around all day watching television, getting medication and attending one group with a case manager that flipped cards. Patients just sat around, played cards and looked forward to going outside for a smoke break. However, due to these facilities transitioning as tobacco free, patients have become more restless and fights often broke out amongst the clients. Further, the other community mental health center had a short term residential and crisis stabilization unit. As an intern, I offered the only counseling sessions for the patients. All of the therapy was given to the outpatient clients; not once did a therapist walk over the short term residential or crisis stabilization unit to conduct therapy with that population. The mental health technicians' facilitated goal and wrap up groups.

On the other hand, the patients with insurance weren't recommended to be transferred out. They would be transferred out only if they brought up that idea. Even if another hospital was more suited to meet their needs, they usually would end up being admitted at our hospital. Some patients requested to be sent to another hospital were ignored if they had insurance. Thus, I would advise you to familiarize yourself with the federal and state laws that explain the concept of transfers.

Eventually, a few months after management implemented the policy of holding uninsured patients in the ER over 12 hours, a patient expressed his grievance to the Agency of Healthcare Administration. AHCA conducted an investigation, and the ER nurse documented that the transfer center refused to admit a patient due to him being uninsured. As a result, the hospital was investigated and fined. Management did not allow that nurse to work in the emergency room behavioral health unit ever again and attempted to act as though they weren't aware of those unethical practices. Thankfully, I wasn't working that day because I would have been the first one corporate and management suspected of "blowing the whistle". I was being scrutinized by management already and the director constantly called me about what I documented in the patient's chart; the director didn't want me to document that management was the reason uninsured patients were held in the ER. Doctors and nurses would express their concern to me about patients being held in the emergency room due to them being uninsured but no one reported it. One physician who worked part time with AHCA told me to report it. However, when you have the reputation of being the employee that challenges unethical practices, coworkers expect you to address every problem all the time. I decided to let it play it out because instinctually I knew it was matter of time before that unethical and illegal practice was uncovered. During the open investigation, we had to attend corporate trainings on the Emtala law which I was already familiar with; however, it was part of the corrective action plan so attendance was mandatory. I didn't call AHCA but I definitely empowered patients/families and gave them the number to AHCA encouraging them to call to file a complaint against the hospital if they felt mistreated or neglected. As stated earlier, the hospital was fined considerably but only for that one case. If AHCA went more in depth with that investigation, went several months back and interviewed employees, my hospital would have been fined substantially. On a positive note, uninsured patients are no longer held for over 12 hours after medical clearance. Also, patients are now given the option to transfer or remain at the hospital.

Overall, sometimes you have to fight injustice indirectly. You don't always have to be on the battlefield putting your name on the line to fight injustice. You can fight indirectly depending on the situation and be just as effective and be thrilled with the results.

Grievances and star cards

During the admission process for patients hospitalized, patients signed a form discussing their right to file grievances and complaints. In the written policy, patients had the right to fill a written grievance. After a while, more patients completed grievances about the poor quality of treatment they received. These written grievance forms were reportedly tracked by the Agency of Healthcare Administration.

After a significant amount of written complaints, the risk manager stated there needs to be action taken to reduce the amount of written grievances. The management advised staff to discontinue giving patients the official grievance form and only give them a blank sheet of paper. I truly did not feel comfortable with this unofficial procedure and continued to give them an official written grievance if they requested one. After patients were constantly writing grievances on blank sheets of paper that were piling into management's box, staff were advised to not even give them a sheet of paper and only verbalize their concerns.

Oftentimes, there would be a patient that was re-admitted and remembered having the option to complete an official written grievance. One male demanded to be given a written grievance. I gave an official grievance to this one patient that was very upset at a nurse. Management e-mailed me about why he was given one. I stated he was given one because it's in the written policy in the admission packet for them to be granted the opportunity to file a written grievance. A week later, management changed the written policy. As a result, patients were no longer able to be given an official grievance form, and I didn’t have the policy that supported me empowering patients. Many patients reported feeling powerless to change how they were maltreated by some staff members.

Ironically, our behavioral health unit had the area’s highest satisfaction scores. In addition, patients were pressured by staff to complete star cards that recognized an employee for doing a great job. I would overhear several staff members telling patients to fill out a star card as well as what positive comments to write on them. The completed star cards were recorded by the hospital patient experience coordinator portraying an image to the public that patients were satisfied with their care.

When hospitals or facilities report great patient satisfaction scores, take that information in with caution. Most patients aren’t even given the opportunity to report anything other what’s desired by the facility. Some patients feel intimidated and only report good experiences especially with an employee standing over them as they complete the survey. Some patients expressed they felt they would be held there longer if they didn’t report satisfaction with their hospital care.

Abuse, neglect and exploitation

There were patients that reported experiencing abuse and neglect on the inpatient behavioral health unit. However, allegations of abuse were rarely reported to the Department of Children and Families or the Agency for Healthcare Administration which investigates those allegations. They were handled internally by risk management. However, if the patient made an allegation against an external assisted living facility or nursing home, staff were mandated to report it to the Department of Children and Families.

Even though there was a huge bulletin with DCF's abuse hotline number above the patient's phones on the wall, some patients were prohibited from using the phones at times. Other patients felt too intimidated to call DCF because any conversations on those phones were within earshot of the nursing station. I would report allegations of abuse or neglect that occurred within and outside of the hospital. Whether or not a case was opened, I uphold my duty as a social worker and mandated reporter to involve DCF in any claims made by patients. Oftentimes, I would be subject to hostility by staff and management. However, if I was in a vulnerable position being maltreated, I hope someone would advocate on my behalf.

Recently, there has been several thefts in the psychiatric emergency room. Several patients have called and reported their valuables not being returned to them. Management and security became involved but nobody was ever held accountable. Half of these patients were brought in unconscious due to an overdose, feeling manic, depressed, or psychotic. As a result, some staff members took advantage of these vulnerable patients. When these patients become stabilized, they become fully aware of missing valuables. One behavioral health technician that was supposed to be taking inventory of valuables stated he didn't feel like walking over to put a patient's jewelry in a safe. This same behavioral health technician always complained about having to pay child support, and most of the thefts occurred while he was working. On the inventory valuable sheet, patients came in with jewelry or money, but somehow it never made it up with the patient to another floor. I would tell patients to report their concerns to hospital administration and if their concerns are dismissed, file a police report.

Also, one patient was not welcomed by the staff on the behavioral health unit. Even though he hasn't been on the unit in a year, he rarely took his medication and talked loudly to himself during his previous admissions which irritated the nurses. He was never aggressive, merely annoying according to several staff members. On one occasion, he was in the emergency room and was medically cleared for admission to the unit. However, as soon as he was brought up there by security, he was not allowed to enter and security had to bring the patient back downstairs. Even though he displayed symptoms of psychosis, he knew he was not wanted on the unit and appeared sad after the nurses refused to open the doors. Eventually, they ended up admitting him since the emergency room doctor put in an admission order before the psychiatrist was able to discharge him from the emergency room. He was transported back upstairs to the unit and discharged within two hours. If nursing staff does not want a particular patient admitted, they will do whatever necessary to block the admission. If that undesirable patient is admitted, that patient is oftentimes discharged the same day whether they benefitted from treatment or not. Hence, society has this perception that more mental health treatment is needed but minimize the importance of the quality of those services rendered.

What to expect from the schedule

Families oftentimes have this perception that their loved ones admitted to the behavioral health unit would be receiving spectacular therapeutic services. But in reality, the program schedule for patients that was displayed on the glass of the nursing station was rarely followed. It would display a program schedule of several therapeutic group activities occurring throughout the day. However, on some days patients only had 1 group; it was normally the psychotherapy group facilitated by the social worker. The nurses and technicians oftentimes did not facilitate groups on a daily basis. As a result, patients just sat, watched TV, slept or lined up at the medication window throughout the day. We would comply with the schedule exactly according to the bulletin when corporate leaders came through, usually once every year. I would see patients constantly walking up to the nursing station viewing this program schedule looking very disappointed.

Psychiatrists

There has been several psychiatrists staffed for our behavioral health unit since the opening. They were smart, wonderful individuals, but different in their approach towards providing care. Each had their flaws but open to make improvements. I've noticed medical providers became so accustomed to assessing patients that they don't take the time to assess their own strengths and weaknesses. One similarity would be that psychiatrists would often prescribe patients the same medication that they had a history of overdosing on.

One psychiatrist would usually meet with his patients for less than one or two minutes and walk off. He would document that he provided psychiatric counseling for 15-30 minutes. So many patients would continuously vent to me about not having enough time with him. It would be brought to his attention on several occasions but he did not modify the time spent meeting with patients. In addition, he would meet with them in the hallway with other patients passing by. Privacy was not an option most of the time for his patients.

Also, a patient's length of stay would depend on the insurance company not really based on the needs of the patient. As soon as the utilization review nurse informed him that the insurance company refused to pay for any more inpatient days, the patient was out the door, suicidal or not. His treatment was so abrupt with the uninsured patients, and some of them were discharged in less than 24 hours.

In addition, he would tell patients that they were being discharged on a certain day. However, if the insurance covered those patients for additional days, he would break his promise and keep them there longer. In addition, he would use his same psychiatric evaluation from a previous admission of a patient and just change the date.

On the other hand, some psychiatrists became too emotionally attached to their patients and seemed to do anything to please and make them happy. In particular, one psychiatrist completed a form stating a female patient was permanently disabled due to her mental illness in an attempt to get her approved for disability. This patient had no history of mental illness and very high functioning. In addition, he would verbally slander the other psychiatrist with his patients.

One psychiatrist wrote a prescription for 200 opiates for a male patient even though the medical doctor decided against it because the patient had a history of opiate dependence and legal convictions for selling his prescription pills. This doctor would sometimes write those type of prescriptions on his prescription pad instead of printing them out on the computer to avoid surveillance by the hospital quality improvement department which monitored discharge medications from doctors. He wouldn’t even document certain medications in his discharge medication list especially if he couldn’t justify giving a patient 2 or more antipsychotics or a high dose of narcotics. Several of those patients discharged with a large amount of medications ended up back in the ER for overdosing where many of them had to be resuscitated. Another psychiatrist was so arrogant and emotionally abused his patients until one patient actually hit him.

Sometimes, a psychiatrist's need to fix patients resulted in patients being arrested or being financially billed unnecessarily for a long length of stay. In particular, one psychiatrist attempted to protect an active duty personnel from the military police. The patient checked himself in for depression. I informed the psychiatrist it would be best for that patient is discharged in 2 days with his officers to avoid legal repercussion. I stated his depression can't be fixed in a few days here. However, the psychiatrist was adamant that he could do a better job of psychiatrically stabilizing him than those psychiatrists on the military base. Even with all those medication changes, the patient stated his depression hasn't changed since his admission.

Unfortunately, after a week of being inpatient, a warrant was issued for his arrest for absconding from the military. The director and psychiatrist requested that the military withdraw the warrant. The military refused stating many officers check themselves into hospitals to avoid consequences. If that psychiatrist had discharged him 2 days earlier, that patient would have avoided going to jail. I'm sure he was even more depressed with that outcome and regretted ever checking into the hospital.

ALFs, pastoral counselors, cab drivers

Patients would request for a chaplain or minister visit to help meet their spiritual needs. Sometimes medication adjustments and psychotherapy alone were not enough for some patients. It was a noticeable positive difference in the patient's mood after receiving pastoral counseling. However, I would request that a patient be seen but sometimes no one showed up. It was a huge disappointment for some patients.

Some patients would remain on the unit awaiting placement into an assisted living facility or adult care home. They would have to be evaluated by the owner or administrator. Sometimes, they would make a commitment to show up and never showed up. When they didn't show, patients would report feeling worse and rejected.

There has been a growing trend among assisted living facilities. They don't want to accept the patient back after being hospitalized but they don't want to relinquish the check either. This one assisted living facility owner would only accept them if they attended a day treatment program daily. She stated they would not be sitting at home wanting her to entertain them.

Unfortunately, our behavioral health unit would usually work solely with this one cab driver because he always showed up hoping to transport patients after being discharged. However, he wouldn't always transport patients to the address given on his cab voucher. In particular, he decided to transport the patient to his son's home instead of the ALF and it was a big dispute that ensued, cops called and the patient was readmitted to the hospital. This same married cab driver kept soliciting female patients to go on dates with him. He knew they were vulnerable and preyed on them. I kept advising staff to not utilize that particular cab driver. However, the other staff didn't care because they felt once that patient is off the unit, that patient's well-being was no longer their responsibility. Eventually after I continued to voice my concerns and another staff member brought it to the attention of management, that cab driver was only allowed to drive males from the hospital.

Rewarded for behavioral problems

As a children’s case manager, I remember working with this one family and my client was a 6yr old boy. I would overhear the patient’s mother telling the psychiatrist in front of the client that he was so bad. When I worked with him, he was very mild mannered. He felt he needed to act bad so they had money in the house; he received disability for his behavioral problems. His check was a great help to the mom because they were finally able to move out of her children’s father home which seemed to be a hostile environment. I’m glad that extra income helped them. However, this child was growing up thinking that misbehaving results in rewards. It may be tolerated as a young child; however, as he ages, that type of defiant oppositional behavior may have legal consequences.

Beware: professional behaving badly

It was very obvious some staff members on the behavioral health unit did not enjoy working in this field, and they fully illustrated their discontent with their career choice through their interactions with patients. Several staff members would be downright verbally abusive to some patients. I overheard one behavioral health technician telling a male patient "stop crying like a woman, you are a man!" One female nurse stated, "Stop all the nonsense, I'm sick of it". One staff member stated "you're older, act like an adult, not a child". One female patient stated to me during psychotherapy that she was in earshot of a behavioral technician stating "I can't wait to take this class so I can get out of this shit hole". I have heard him make comments like that on several occasions but I wasn't expecting a patient to hear it and share it with the rest of the group members. It took me so much time calming down a group of angry patients during group therapy when staff members would cut patients deep with their words. However, it wasn't balanced because patients arguing back with staff usually resulted in them being held against their will even longer. The staff usually would document the patient's behaviors but not the precipitating factors that caused the patient to react.

Some staff members were very sexually inappropriate. The behavior technicians and nurses would reprimand patients against inappropriate touching and holding of hands. However, those same male technicians would be in the nursing station giving back massages to the female nurses. One day I was about to walk into the nourishment room, and the nurse manager was bent over with a male technician standing behind her pressed against her buttocks. He looked at me as I quietly closed the door back. After rumors began circulating about her having sex with the technician she supervised, she sent an email threatening employees about gossip. Interestingly, she normally sits there as coworkers' gossip but it only became a problem when she became the object of discussion. She later resigned and ended up dating another male behavioral technician.

One male technician asked a female patient if he could wash her back in the shower; he actually ended up having sex with another former female patient after he was fired for stealing. He was ordering food trays for patients that were already discharged. He was also stealing items from patients during his inventory checks through their belongings. Several patients reported that their money and valuables were missing but their concerns were rarely taken seriously due some of them deemed as incompetent by the psychiatrist. In particular, a sharp witted female patient was being discharged and noticed her jewelry was missing. I gave her the number to the patient experience coordinator who visited the unit interrogating staff about her jewelry. Interesting, that technician miraculously found it and returned it to her.

Some of the employees that worked for environmental services would transport linens to the unit. However, I caught one of them stealing snacks purchased for patients out of the nourishment room. On a different occasion, he came in bragging he's getting ready to rob the nourishment room, and one of the technicians gave him some snacks. I definitely addressed that issue with my coworker.

Some staff members would fall asleep or be too preoccupied on their cell phones while supervising patients. Room checks and rounding in the hallway as directed were not being completed. As a result, patients were having sex. Some patients were later caught doing drugs because employees weren't thoroughly checking their belongings. One patient escaped through the back exit.

Privacy and confidentiality

Some outpatient counselors would bring in their family member to their office while clients were in their office discussing their problems. In particular, I witnessed an outpatient counselor's spouse eavesdropping during an individual session. Another instance of a violation of privacy occurred in the emergency room. Some doctors speak so loudly to certain patients discussing their illnesses which had a social stigma to it without regards to other patients being within earshot of that discussion. In addition, one male mental health technician took out his cell phone laughing and began recording a patient that was exhibiting active symptoms of psychosis. He was consequently fired later that week; however, he had already shown his fiancé and others of that patient's mental breakdown. Also, sometimes staff would disclose a patient's admission to the behavioral health unit without their consent. Sometimes, patients were given the discharge instructions and prescriptions designated for other patients.

Oftentimes, doctors with no privileges at your hospital will be given preferential treatment. In particular, a patient's father was sitting in the nursing station chatting with the charge nurse and regular nurse. I asserted he could not be sitting there with other patients' confidential information in plain view of him.

Medically cleared

Patients are oftentimes medically cleared in the emergency room even though no lab work or urine screens were even completed. If that patient was causing an uproar in the ER, the ER wanted them moved right away. One female patient on the behavioral health unit had a horrible infestation of pubic lice that the nurses didn't find out until the day of discharge; however, staff claimed to be performing skin checks upon admission. In addition, several patients had to be rushed to the medical floors because they were medially inappropriate for a behavioral health unit. Some geriatric patients were just not appropriate and would have been better cared for on a medical floor with the psychiatrist being consulted and providing care for them.

Some patients were prematurely medically cleared and ultimately had to be transferred to a medically floor due to health issues being overlooked. Even though a patient is medically cleared, there may still some be concerns about a medical issue. As a result, a consult would be put in for a nurse specialist or physician specialist to evaluate the patient. However, some doctors did not even want to visit patients on the behavioral health floor. I overhead a group of physicians entering the unit stating "I can't stand coming here seeing these crazies". As a result of these attitudes, the physical health of patients became compromised. In particular, one patient had a wound consult put in but no wound care nurse came to see the patient until several days later after the infection began spreading. That patient could have died because the primary focus for those behavioral health nurses are psychiatric, and medical needs are secondary. Oftentimes behavioral health nursing staff are assessing symptoms of mental illness, not accurately assessing the physical health decline of their patients. Hence, physicians should carefully determine if a patient would be better served on a medical floor versus a behavioral health unit.

Also, I've witnessed some medical doctors refusing to admit to a medical floor mentally ill patients and arguing for them to be admitted directly to behavioral health. Sometimes, the psychiatrist would refuse to admit the patient directly to the behavioral health unit after reviewing their medical condition. As a result, the patients would have to be held in the ER overnight until morning until one of those physicians changed their mind due to pressure from administration.

One patient under voluntary baker act status was placed in the ER behavioral health unit and had a blood glucose of over 400. His vital signs and blood sugar wasn't monitored for nearly 12 hours during the night shift. I came in the next morning and asked the nurse and paramedic to check his blood sugar, and discovered it was approaching 500. After I expressed my concerns, he was given some fluids and insulin to lower his blood sugar to prevent him from going into a diabetic coma. Hence, medically clearance doesn't always mean that a patient is medically stable so closely monitor their physical health as well.

Assisted living facilities

I encourage all family members to visit an assisted living facility before allowing your loved one to be sent there from the hospital. As a social worker, I didn't know of the condition of these assisted living facilities. I was just given a flyer and sometimes only a listing in a community resource guide but had to send patients either there or a homeless shelter. I was never allowed the opportunity to visit ALFs during working hours. I could describe what to expect about placement in regards to cost but that was about it. Unfortunately, an elderly male was attacked by a guy that snuck into the unlocked facility where I had sent other patients for placement. In addition, an assisted living facility owner was sent to prison for stealing patients' medications and disability checks. Thus, visit the facilities and research them.

Outpatient Substance Abuse Agencies & Audits

I worked as an evaluator and outpatient counselor for one of the biggest substance abuse treatment centers in the county. Outpatient programs receive money from various funding sources, and my agency wanted to keep money flowing to our agency. The majority of the clients entering into the program were either court ordered, had an open case child protective investigations, on probation, or referred by driving under the influence programs. There was pressure from management to graduate clients to improve successful outcomes for the agency thus proving to the funders how effective our agency was towards improving the lives of our clients. However, there was so much deception in what was reported to the courts and funders. We were instructed that patients didn't even have to finish treatment successfully. They were to be discharged successfully as long as their fee balance was $0. Even if clients missed drug urine screens because of a relapse, we were to assume that the drug screen would be negative.

The counselors were also told to improve outcomes by not coding clients as unemployed even if they were jobless. They were to be coded as homemakers in their discharge. Some counselors were instructed to go back about 3 months and change all the discharges of individuals from being unemployed to employed.

In addition, the agency received more money from patients in residential programs.

As a result, some patients were evaluated and recommended for residential treatment even if they didn’t meet criteria of needing that level of care. Those clients would complete residential treatment and then have to complete outpatient afterwards.

There was so much pressure to collect money from patients if they were paying out of pocket for treatment. I remember receiving an email from the vice president about fee collections. No clients were to be successfully discharged if they had an outstanding balance. It didn’t matter how many treatment groups a client attended or how well they abstained from alcohol or illicit drug use. A client normally was expected to attend treatment for 3 months; however, if that patient paid their balance in less than a month, they were successfully discharged.

Ordinarily, a group facilitator would pass around one sign in sheet for participants to sign in. However, I had to use two sign in sheets for the groups I facilitated because the agency wasn’t supposed to be billing clients with Medicaid and the Department of Children and Families at the same time. Two sign in sheets gave the impression that two separate groups were being conducted. However, all of those clients were placed in one group room at the same time receiving the same treatment. Also, some of those drug urine screens weren’t random especially if the counselor had the power to go into the system and change the date and times of urine screens.

In addition, there was an HIV program component that generated a significant amount of money for the program. It provided counseling services for clients diagnosed with HIV. The HIV counselors would visit my clients in outpatient and facilitate a group once every one or two months. They would bill for an hour and 30 minutes even though they would only stay for 20 minutes showing the clients a video. They would be caught being dishonest with their billing practices because many patients would do a urine drug screen before group. As a result, the times conflicted in the service activity logs. How could a patient be in a group at 6:00pm if that patient was submitting to random drug screen at 6:05pm?

Also, everyone should have the right to decline HIV testing. However, to get the HIV program numbers up, clients in other programs weren't even given the option to submit for an HIV test. It was mandatory because the agency wanted to keep employees on payroll even though some of them were just sitting in their office with nothing to do.

The conflict I had with the staff of this program was the fact that they weren't culturally sensitive. All of the posters on the doors of those staff members portrayed only black men as the face of HIV. I walked down that hall and realized there wasn't any other race, ethnicity or gender represented. I brought it to the attention of one of the counselors, and she attempted to justify their actions by referencing statistics. I responded that I wasn't impressed by statistics because statistics historically have been utilized to identify a problem not a positive quality with black men. I was about to send an email addressing my concern to the CEO, managers, and directors.

However, when I reported to work one morning, the posters were no longer displayed on the exterior part of their doors. I didn't see them as I walked down the hallway. I felt better because I didn't know what the outcome would have been for me if I had sent that email. Interesting enough, those posters weren't taken down completely but were taped on the interior of the doors. I decided to leave that issue alone because what my co-workers put inside their office wasn't my concern. Thus, you have to pick and choose your battles to preserve your energy for the battles that may lie ahead.

Also, I've noticed that at the mental health and substance abuse programs I've worked for, we always had an advance notice of chart audit. Either we would pick our charts that we desired to be audited or be given a list charts that would be pulled. We would always have enough time fix them up to meet standards. If agencies that monitor these programs performed more random audits, they would probably get a more accurate picture of the true condition of these programs. These providing facilities would do more to adhere to providing quality services to clients.

Language barriers

Patients that didn't speak any English rarely benefitted from treatment. There were several Spanish speaking patients admitted on the behavioral health unit but there weren't any employees that worked in the daytime that spoke Spanish. We would use an interpreter phone to complete a psychosocial or nursing assessment. The Spanish speaking only patients would be encouraged to attend groups but they didn't understand a word that was spoken. How could they truly benefit from the therapeutic group interventions? Luckily on occasions, there would be another Spanish speaking patient that offered to translate during psychotherapy groups.

I would print out educational handouts in Spanish for the patient to read. If there is a large segment of the population that speaks a foreign language in that area, management should hire a translator for that particular population at least during the daytime so all patients can receive equal therapeutic treatment. It's impossible to be able to have a translator for every foreign language. However, if there is a large number of patients from a specific culture utilizing therapeutic services, then their language should be the one worth investing in. For the hearing impaired, there is a sign language interpreter that is present throughout the course of that patient's length of stay.

For consumers

In conclusion, my hope is that readers found an experience of mine helpful in deciding whether to pursue mental health and substance abuse treatment as a career choice or treatment option. I've seen an increase in advertisements for psychiatric medications and treatment facilities. Society appears to be increasing awareness about mental illness and motivating folks to seek treatment. I think mental health awareness is wonderful because people that truly need therapeutic help are less ashamed to reach out for it. However, the general public should also be informed of the harm that may result from receiving treatment. Some patients leave with more problematic symptoms that were not present when they first arrived to treatment. Some patients reported developing a drug dependency as a result of poor medication management by the psychiatrists. If that psychiatrist is only interested in managing the symptoms of mental illness but overlooking addictive properties of certain medications, then oftentimes that patient was more likely to overdose. Some patients were able to recover fully from an overdose and some were less fortunate.

Sometimes, a psychiatrist will adjust medications during a patient's hospitalization because insurance companies decline to pay for continuous inpatient treatment unless a medication is changed. Oftentimes, the medication prescribed was therapeutic but additional medications may be added if the psychiatrist doesn't feel comfortable discharging the patient yet. That's why you have so many patients on so many medications during their hospitalization and not given a prescription for some of them upon discharge.

Many family members would get frustrated with their relatives that received inpatient or outpatient treatment; patients ended up returning home the same way they entered treatment with no positive progress. However, the problem doesn't always lie with the patient, sometimes it's the program. I would advise you to ask your loved one that's receiving therapeutic intervention to describe their typical day on an inpatient behavioral health unit or outpatient program. Make sure you follow up with the director of the unit if the posted schedule isn't matching up with their reported daily experiences.

Also, if possible write down important contact phone numbers before you are transported to an inpatient mental health facility. Most people in modern society just rely on cellphones and don't memorize important phone numbers. Unfortunately, some phones are lost during transport or in the emergency room. In addition, you will likely be flagged as confidential; if family members or friends were to call to hospital inquiring about you, they will be told you're not there or unable to confirm or deny your admission to the hospital.

Furthermore, if you have your cellphone with you, ask staff members for a piece of paper and pencil to write numbers down before they seal your phone in a valuables bag. It is extremely important for patients to reconnect with their loved ones through phone calls. Most folks want to feel as though their absence from home matters and that they are deeply missed.

Many mental health facilities have certain visitation hours for family members and friends to spend time with their loved ones. It can be quite understandable that there needs to be some regulation to monitor people coming in and out of the locked unit for safety and security. In particular, one female visitor kept attempting to sneak illicit drugs to her boyfriend that was a male patient. In addition, some patients have heated verbal exchanges with visitors and those visitors have to be escorted out. As a result, not all visits are therapeutic.

For the most part, visitation by loved ones motivate patients to make the most during their recovery to be the best version of themselves for their family and friends after discharge. Unfortunately, many people that work full time are unable to come visit during specific visitation hours. However, I always advise patients and loved ones to ask the attending psychiatrist to put in an order for a special visitation time outside of standard visitation hours because family involvement is a necessary component of most patients' treatment plan.

Also, if that loved one is receiving outpatient counseling or case management, take time to review that bill. Sometimes case managers are billing for 2-3 hours and only providing 20-30 minutes of services. Also, if you are going week after week for counseling and not really benefiting from it, then simply ask that counselor to give you names of other providers. Now we counselors may be initially offended, but ultimately we want what’s best for our patient. If we can’t give it, we hope somebody else can.

Hence, the benefits of receiving mental health and substance abuse treatment definitely outweighs the risks of not receiving help at all if you need it. I’ve seen some miraculous breakthroughs for several patients. I’ve noticed that patients that were prescribed one or two very effective medications seemed to respond better to treatment than patients prescribed over ten psychiatric medications. Sometimes less can be better, and more medication doesn’t always equate with better results.

Even if the medication or therapy wasn’t effective, some patients reported receiving great insight from fellow patients in the program during group that was positively life changing. Staff members often encourage patients to interact with one another resulting in close-knit bonds. As a result of these bonds, some patients want to remain in contact with one another after being discharged. However, I would advise against interactions amongst patients after discharge. Patients often present one way in a structured environment with twenty-four hour supervision but often change their attitude and behavior once they are released. Several patients came back expressing to me about negative and violent encounters with former patients they linked up with after being discharged from an inpatient behavioral health unit.

In addition, patients reported having bad experiences with friendships they developed in an outpatient setting. You really don't know the inner motivation of the patient sitting next to you seeking treatment. One patient in my substance abuse outpatient counseling group was a criminal informant. I didn't know he was because he was mandated to the program in an effort to retain custody of his kids. However, he decided to make some money too after befriending another client that was still selling drugs. The criminal informant stated he was awarded nearly 10,000 dollars. The patient he set up called me from jail angry about how it turned out.

Important to note, people that visit a primary care physician are asked to fill out a patient health questionnaire. Most patients just answer the questions and overlook the section at the top which puts a timeframe, such as in the last week, two weeks or twenty-four hours. One of the questions ask if they've experienced suicidal thoughts, and some patients check yes without realizing the results could be interpreted as current thoughts of suicide. Hence, make sure you look carefully at the directions even if it's in smaller print than the questions. There has been an increase in patients sent to the emergency room from their primary care physicians after completing these surveys due to a misunderstanding.

Also, one of the toughest decisions most family members or friends must make after they've done all that they can do is making alternate home living arrangements for their loved one. If a relative that lives with you has a persistent severe mental illness or chemical dependency disorder and continues to become violent towards you even while on psychotropic medications, it may be your best interest to take him or her to the hospital. Allow that hospital place them in an assisted living facility, group home, boarding home, or adult care home after you've visited the address of the facility.

In particular, there was this bald, tall and big adult male who had a history of violence against his elderly mother, law enforcement and recently threatened to kill his father due to paranoia. They dropped him off to the emergency room, and I advised them to not let him back in their home. My intuition and spiritual consciousness was speaking so loudly that something tragic was going to happen to them if he returned home. I advised them to let his placement fall upon the shoulders of hospital social workers and discharge planners. It's less work for hospital staff to send him back home instead of finding a different placement for him so hospital staff usually attempt to convince family members to allow patients to return back home. However, I reminded the parents that the patient received a disability check and therefore had a monthly income, so other placement options could be explored.

While on the inpatient behavioral health unit, the patient was compliant with medication and displayed no aggressive behaviors. The parents ultimately decided to take him back home. It's quite understandable that they would want their adult son back home with them because they love him. Unfortunately, within a few hours he stabbed his elderly father and nearly killed him. That father had to be rushed to the hospital immediately, and the patient went to jail.

Hence, don't just rely on feedback from hospital staff about the behavior of a patient during their hospitalization. Some people are on their best behavior in the presence of strangers while in an unfamiliar environment. Take into consideration your prior experiences with that family member who has demonstrated violence. Balance your experiences, the hospital's point of view, and your loved one's preference for placement in order to make the best decision that will keep you and your loved ones safe.

Most important, if you are presenting to the hospital with a medical problem, make sure that is the primary focus of treatment. Oftentimes the doctors will look at a past medical records. If there is documentation a history of a mental health diagnosis, they may minimize your concerns about your physical health. Further, some patients with no history of mental illness are diagnosed with a mental diagnosis if the physician can't find anything after reviewing initial laboratory results. In particular, one patient reported having parasites in his stomach and intestines.

However, he was deemed as psychotic and placed on a mental health hold. However, while on the medical floor, further medical testing was done and it was discovered that the patient did indeed have parasites. The patient never exhibited signs of psychosis; however, it seems preferable to label a patient with a wrong diagnosis than to acknowledge not knowing the true cause of the presenting medical problem.

Overall, there are some great healthcare professionals that genuinely enjoy this line of work and are very knowledgeable about mental health and substance abuse. However, if by chance you encounter clinical providers that treat you poorly, it’s important to not be discouraged. Trust me, as you continue to persevere in your pursuit for the right therapist, psychiatrist or program, eventually you’ll be able to find what you need. Sometimes, therapy without medication is best for some patients. Other patients just need medication management and therapy isn’t needed. Some patients need a combination of both to be their best self. Further, some patients don’t need any medication or therapy but have convinced themselves something is wrong or have allowed others to persuade them into entering treatment. Sometimes, just taking time each day for self-reflection and discovery about their thoughts, feelings, and behaviors may be all the intervention they need. There are also other avenues to receive the healing one needs including inspirational books, free support groups, or a crisis counseling hotline.

Tips for providers

Please remember to always stay balanced. When I lost my state of inner peace on occasions, nothing would go right for me on the job. Once you're balanced, you can handle any unforeseen challenges that await you in this helping profession. Meditate before, during, and after work even if it's just for 5 minutes.

You will definitely encounter workplace conflicts. I've had numerous visits with human resources, corporate, and directors for challenging unethical practices but I've always left each meeting with the victory. In addition, I've had several co-workers conspiring against me in the conference room. I could hear their conversation since my office was next to the conference room with only a thin wall separating the two offices. I've worked in some very hostile environments. Being connected with my feelings, staying true to my intentions for working in this field, and maintaining my peace helped me to keep my sanity.

For a year, I was the only clinical social worker on the behavioral health unit and performed all of the psychosocial assessments and discharge planning for all the patients. Even though I worked around healthcare professionals, most of them did not demonstrate caring attitudes towards me during that time frame. However, most of them didn't fully understand all the work that had to be completed on my end. Now there are 3 full time social workers and 2-3 interns to perform the same tasks I completed alone. At the boot camp, I was the only counselor for nearly 70 young adolescents when prior to my arrival there were 4 counselors managing those 70 clients. In the substance abuse outpatient program, I managed a caseload of 50-60 while some counselors a case load ranging from 3-10 clients. Hence, there will be times when your job will overwhelm you with work. However, it's during those tough times that your clinical skills will expand in ways you never thought possible.

Patients that have insurance and are admitted but denied coverage during their behavioral health inpatient hospitalization seem to be getting billed significantly. As a result, the utilization reviewer and intake should communicate with that patient when that coverage ends, especially at a for profit mental health facility. Some patients will desire to check themselves out early and enroll in an outpatient program to avoid unnecessary costs. As a member of a particular insurance plan, it will benefit you greatly to call or have a relative call on your behalf advocating for extended coverage before the last cover day. Some patients and family members may not care about the financial costs during a path to wellness at the moment.

However, some patients have been billed $40,000 to $100,000 after being hospitalized 2-4 days beyond their last day of insurance coverage. Unfortunately, one of the triggers for several patients having mental breakdowns are financial stressors. A patient being released from a mental health facility just to be feeling worse a week or two later when the inflated hospital bill arrives is not a desirable outcome. This negative occurrence can be a huge setback towards a patient maintaining his/her mental health stability.

If an assisted living facility or adult care home is trying to get a patient out of their facility, they will oftentimes drop them off at the hospital and leave. Typically, they are obligated to take that patient back if they are medically stable or if the patient poses no harm to other residents. On the other hand, if that patient is troublesome and his/her behaviors are more of a nuisance, they may convince a family members to pick up the patient and instruct them to take them to the hospital. At that point, that family member is responsible for that patient so that assisted living facility can refuse to accept the patient back. My advice to family members is that if you know your relative's current placement keeps reporting problems they are encountering with your relative, be wary of any requests to pick up that patient and take them off the premises. While they are residing in that facility, the patient must remain in that facility until an alternative placement has been found. However, if you pick up that patient, the patient may have to stay at home with you while you explore various housing options for your loved one. Thus, review the policies and laws about the circumstances that would give a facility the right to refuse re-admitting a client.

You may encounter some inpatient clients that lack patience and demand that you accommodate them right away. I've had patients banging on my office violently demanding to be discharged; things were getting so out of control that my director had to put a black tint over the rectangular glass window over my office door. During an outpatient counseling group, I had one client aggressively confront me about making payments to the agency for treatment. Important to note, whenever you have a client verbally attack you in a room with several clients, you have to stand up for yourself. In a split second, I visually scanned the faces of the other clients.

If I wasn't as assertive with him as he was with me, I would have lost respect from every client in that room. If you don't have their respect, you definitely won't be able to engage them in the therapeutic process. I didn't ignore his comment but acknowledged his frustration and asserted that the agency is a business. You have to know the specific population you're working with, and sometimes being too nice and soft-spoken is not therapeutic. You have to know when to be firm and look a rude patient directly in their eyes without blinking.

Further, be mindful of the hidden intentions of family members that make reports to law enforcement or physicians. In particular, one elderly patient's daughter reported to law enforcement that her father hit her with a pool stick and it broke in half. However, during my interview with her she admitted that he never hit her and she just wanted him placed in an assisted living facility. Some people will lie when they really want someone out of their lives so it's so important to value what the patient is stating as well.

On a different note, some concerns by family members must be taken more seriously. This patient's mother found her teenage son naked covered in his blood after he had hung himself. He was admitted to the behavioral health unit and discharged in less than 2 days. He was never seen by the therapist for individual therapy even though the insurance companies are misled to believe that type of service is occurring. The mother of this patient called the social worker and left a message stating that her son will manipulate to get out the hospital faster. She pleaded stating her son was not ready to be discharged. However, he was discharged without speaking with her even though she was his healthcare representative. In less than three weeks, that patient hung himself and found by his mother again. Any patient that is young and impulsive, get as much family or friend collateral information as possible and take what they report seriously.

Some of these patients admitted to behavioral health units are billed as self-paying clients even though they have insurance. Registration workers are often nervous and apprehensive about meeting with anyone presenting with psychiatric issues. As a result, they will classify them as uninsured or even use their old insurance information from a previous visit years ago. Most patients have their insurance cards. Insurance companies require prior authorization for inpatient behavioral health care. If an initial request isn't completed within a timely manner, that request for authorization is denied. The patient ends up being discharged and billed even though it due to negligence by hospital staff members. Most of these patients report financial problems as a stressor so just make sure registration is not overlooking patients presenting with psychiatric illness. I would oftentimes make a copy of the insurance card or contact family members per the patient's consent to obtain insurance information so I could complete a prior authorization. Those hospital bills are very expensive so if we can assist to eliminate them for a patient then it's worth the additional effort to verify their insurance even if registration chooses not to.

When exiting and entering a locked inpatient mental health facility, make sure patients are not walking out behind you without your knowledge. As you close a door, pull the handle to ensure it securely closes. In particular, one female patient quietly walked out of the emergency room behavioral health holding section. It wasn't realized that she had escaped until about five minutes later. As soon as environmental services staff left, she walked out behind them. The door was not secure and never had been completely repaired despite numerous work order requests. She was later found by the charge nurse walking on a main road and consequently brought back to the emergency room. Thus, just be mindful that you are being watched as you exit and enter, and patients that are held against their will want their freedom back. Another patient wanting to be released immediately snatched the employee badge from a nurse and tried to leave. Hence, keep your employee badge out of arm's reach; it may be helpful to place it in your pocket or inside your white jacket after you've shown it for identification purposes.

Sometimes patients with active police warrants are brought into the emergency room behavioral health holding section. Communication between night and day shift is so critical to ensure that patients are discharged into police custody. For instance, one patient had several active warrants and the police officer instructed the day shift nurse to notify law enforcement before he was discharged. However, this patient wasn't medically discharge until later that night. The night shift nurse was printing out the discharge instructions so I politely reminded them that the patient had an active arrest warrant. The night shift nurse stated he had no idea about the arrest warrant and was just about to walk the patient out of the hospital. He stated the day shift nurse just discussed the medical aspects of the patients but failed to include the legal component. Hence, it's important to inquire about legal holds for patients during shift report.

On the other hand, communication between staff members on inpatient behavioral health units have occurred but patients weren't not informed about pending legal charges. The reason why most patients were not informed that they will be taken into custody upon discharge is because there was a pattern of patients reporting suicidal thoughts the day of discharge after they became aware arrest warrants. Thus, the treatment team should make a determination on a case by case basis if it will be in the patient's best interest to inform them of a police hold. Some patients can receive therapy to help them cope with being brought into police custody and have people in place to bail them out. However, some patients will never mentally prepared to be taken into police custody and it may be more appropriate to just walk them out completely unaware of officers waiting outside of the unit doors.

Important to note, some physicians, nursing, and medical personnel utilize the involuntary mental health hold to force medical treatment and prevent patients from signing out against medical advice. Most of these patients are competent and have the right to decline medical interventions if they are not a danger to themselves and their lives aren't in serious jeopardy. However, sometimes staff panic when certain patients want to leave and hold those patients in the hospital involuntarily even though the primary goal is for medical not mental health or substance abuse treatment. If a patient is declining certain medical procedures while they are under a substance abuse or mental illness legal hold, a psychiatrist should be consulted immediately to determine competency and a patient advocate or health care representative should be allowed to advocate for the patient as well. The ethics and compliance officer should be consulted and any staff member can call the ethics hotline if there is a concern about whether treatment methods are appropriate.

Following up with patient after they've been discharged from inpatient is crucial to the continuous recovery and stability. Asking patients if they have experienced any barriers with their outpatient providers or pharmacies for their medications. Sometimes prescriptions are sent electronically to the wrong pharmacy, or some medications have high co-pays that the patient didn't anticipate. It's important to anticipate potentials barriers and have a solution for them. The majority of patients felt as though the follow up call from intake inquiring about their wellbeing not only in a hospital setting but also outside of it made them feel as though they still mattered. However, the follow up call is not the time to engage the patient in therapy; refer that work to their outpatient provider that will be providing care on a continuous basis.

Some patients were sent as a direct admission to the inpatient behavioral health unit and had no idea what to expect once they voluntarily signed in. Before they signed in, I would take time to explain to them that once they signed in, they would have to be discharged by the psychiatrist and couldn't just walk out against medical advice on a secure locked facility. It's important to explain thoroughly to patients with no prior inpatient behavioral health hospitalization as much as possible about the unit, items prohibited, freedoms taken away, the pros and cons so they can make an informed decision. People don't like to feel manipulated into signing themselves into a locked unit or blindsided by what to expect so it's best to offer as much knowledge available.

Also, if you work as intake, you'll get calls throughout the day. Some people will call requesting information about your facility or community resources. On the other hand, some callers will call intoxicated threatening to commit suicide. One caller stated "I'm going to kill myself and it's your fault! What is your name and you're not getting mine". My response was call 911 or come to the hospital emergency room. Further, if that person keeps making harassing and threatening phone calls, make sure your voicemail offers the local crisis hotline, 911 and advises them to go to the nearest hospital in emergencies.

In addition, some people would come into the hospital emergency room, declined to check in and requested only to speak with me. I would respectfully decline those requests brought to my attention by other emergency room staff members. If you can't document in the medical record on that person, I would advise you not to speak with them. They can walk out even after you've given them resources and do something to hurt themselves; you will be viewed as their last point of contact with a healthcare provider. You don't want that liability especially when you have nothing documented that a conversation ever took place. I decided to give copies of a community resource guide to the receptionist at the front to give to people just wanting information so they wouldn't have to check in and get billed.

Important to note, pay attention to your surroundings when venting about patients to your co-workers. When I was a case manager, I was in the office and overheard a therapist in the adjacent office speaking negatively about a patient and her children. He called her "dumb" and the children "dirty". He was talking so loudly so I decided to ask him to lower his voice. As I stepped outside my office, I saw a little kid standing at the doorway of the therapists' office listening to that therapist venting. I went inside that therapist's office, closed the door behind me and asked him to lower his voice. That therapist became upset that I asked him to lower his voice and to not insult patients. It's quite common for staff to discuss their cases with other staff to seek clarity and possible solutions on how to deal with a situation. However, some therapists attain a hearty laugh at the expense of others and exploit the problematic issues of their clients. Unfortunately, some therapists or counselors are so accustomed to giving advice and pointing out the flaws in others, but they'll refuse to acknowledge their own errors of judgment.

Some patients sent to the hospital by law enforcement or ambulance are at their baseline and function at that level. They have had years of inpatient behavioral health hospitalizations with no evidence of improvement indicating a personality disorder. Some patients are chronically suicidal. Others can be manipulative by threatening suicide if they don't get admitted and ultimately misuse the services. Most patients are diagnosed with a diagnosis the insurance will pay for such as bipolar, depressive or schizophrenia even though some patients truly are antisocial or malingering.

Some patients are placed on an involuntary hold for behavioral health even though it's clearly substance abuse impairment. Many people say things they don't mean under the influence of alcohol or another illicit substance. It's important for the patient to be medically stabilized in the emergency room. Reassess them after the alcohol or illicit substance impairment dissipates to determine if they truly need to be admitted on a behavioral health unit.

Important to note, some medical personnel do not review the involuntary forms that hold a patient against their will. One patient was brought in by ambulance but as I reviewed the form, the support living coach crossed out law enforcement and wrote her name. I gave her the benefit of the doubt because she might not have had the form for licensed professionals and used the one for law enforcement. I looked up her name on the state's website to verify a license of physician, mental health counselor, social worker or psychiatrist, and she had no license. I called her informing her that it's against the law to pose as a law enforcement or licensed professional. The involuntary hold was invalid, so I informed the physician that the patient could not be held against her will. The patient was discharged back to her group home. Thus, it's so important to verify badge numbers of law enforcement or license numbers of healthcare professionals. Anyone can print out forms off the internet and complete a form under false pretense and have someone involuntary held against their will. Hence, it's crucial to thoroughly examine legal documents.

In particular, medical residents were completing involuntary Baker Act forms and weren't licensed. On the form, it clearly states that providers have to be licensed. Patients were being held against their will on the medical floors and denied the right to sign themselves out against medical advice. I caught this problem when I reviewed an involuntary professional certificate for the baker act and noticed that the medical resident wrote her name where the patient's name should have been. Secondly, the form didn't have a date, time, or criteria defined by the statute to warrant an involuntary hold of a patient. I addressed it with management and medical residents were no longer able to complete involuntary holds on patients due to mental illness because they weren't licensed to exercise that authority.

Being attentive and soft spoken seemed very effective during one to one interactions. Trust me, you will develop the skills to manage problematic situations as long as you are paying attention to your surroundings but mostly importantly to the reaction within yourself.

Overall, if you feel no other career choice could give you fulfilment, then I would encourage you to enter or remain in the mental health and substance abuse treatment field. You are destined to do great. Always seek out a mentor that has experienced challenges. Some mentors will focus on their triumphs only but you also need someone to reveal their painful learning experiences as well. You don’t have to be perfect, just be the best that you can be. My flaws turned out to be my greatest assets. Having combination skin, being thin, having a slight limp due to deep vein thrombosis and a geographic tongue evident every time I spoke allowed my patients/clients to feel comfortable sharing with me their insecurities and problems since mine were clearly evident. In addition, my personal struggles with depression, anxiety, and low self-esteem gave me the insight to recognize those symptoms in others and providing individual and group therapy were my strengths. Thus, a physical attribute, painful/shameful experience, or personality flaw can be used by God who can transform that perceived weakness into an undeniable, terrific asset in this field.

Further, I’ve definitely learned that every battle can’t be fought. Sometimes it’s best to walk away from certain situations. No program, clinician or doctor can be perfect. However, if there are minor changes that can be made that would result in better patient experiences, then it’s worth fighting for. It is important to articulate valid concerns but equally as important to offer effective solutions. I was able to successfully implement positive changes over time with God, the help of great new leaders in management, attentive psychiatrists willing to modify their practice, dynamic and receptive medical residents, personable and understanding medical physicians, and awesome co-workers. The good experiences definitely outweighed the bad experiences. Overall, I'm hoping that there will be at least a discussion about an experience of mine amongst leaders that are in a position to implement positive change affecting individuals beyond my reach. I also hope my shared experiences are comforting to those in the field on the verge of giving up. Trust me, it can and will get better.

Acknowledgments

I would like to thank God first & foremost for helping me to maintain my peace of mind! I'm grateful for my parents, Barbara and Howard Coleman Sr., and sister Katarsha for being a listening ear, giving unconditional love, & offering words of encouragement. I'm forever grateful to inspirational Oprah Winfrey for helping me gain valuable insight about myself. I'm very appreciative of my best friends Harry Jr., Guerdy, and Jacinta for being there for me. Special thanks to cousins Shanona for being supportive and Antwon for the great times on vacation. Special thanks to my eldest cousin Herbert Moon Jr for being a ray of sunshine and source of laughter. Thanks to my uncle David & wife Deitra, aunt Jeraldine, uncle Ben & wife Edna, Aunt Barbara Ann & uncle Stewart, Aunt Elaine & uncle Eli, aunt Jack, uncle Sam & aunt Elaine. Much appreciation to cousins Glenn, Wenona, Lowana, Kynjuana, Ira, Lester, Daron, Derrick, Adrian, Latoia, Earl, and niece Kamyah. In loving memory of Grandma Lorene who offered pearls of wisdom which truly helped me with on the job challenges. In loving memory of Grandma Lottie Mae for our great times sitting, eating, and laughing on the porch. Special thanks to godmothers Olive & Anita. I'm grateful to my intern supervisor Michelle V., teachers Ronald & Juanita, & my church family. I am appreciative of phenomenal playwright Tyler Perry for his great advice. Most importantly, thank you readers!

Howard Coleman Jr serves currently as a registered nurse, certified addiction professional, licensed clinical social worker, and mental health awareness trainer for medical physicians/residents. He wrote this book with the intention of providing valuable insight that will positively influence others. He was born and raised in Fort Pierce, FL attending Lincoln Park Academy and moved to Tampa, FL to attend the University of South Florida and Hillsborough Community College. He is a member of Alpha Phi Alpha Fraternity Inc., National Association of Social Workers, and Psi Chi Honor Society in Psychology.

Other work by author: *Speaking Skin*

Facebook: Howard Coleman

Instagram: howardcolemanjr

e-mail: howardjr2010@hotmail.com

www.ingramcontent.com/pod-product-compliance
Lightning Source LLC
Chambersburg PA
CBHW050051060826
49398CB00033B/463

* 9 7 8 1 7 2 6 3 6 6 6 3 2 *

Praise for *Journaling as a Spiritual Practice*

This book is a gift to anyone walking through sorrow, anxiety, or spiritual disorientation. If you've known journaling could help you through your journey but have stared at a blank page and wondered where on earth to begin, this is the book you've been waiting for. Drawing on her training in therapeutic and spiritual journaling as well as her own lived experience of "sorrow upon sorrow," Allison Byxbe offers a practical, compassionate guide for meeting God on the page and turns journaling from an intimidating solo activity into a warm invitation to sit with Jesus and your own story. In these pages you'll find simple how-tos, honest personal reflections, and thoughtful prompts that make it natural to put pen to page and discover, line by line, that God really is with you. *Journaling as a Spiritual Practice* will encourage beginners and long-time journalers alike.

Ann Voskamp, *New York Times* bestselling author of *One Thousand Gifts* and *WayMaker*

I have to be one of the least likely candidates to write a review on a book about journaling! I've been on numerous journaling "kicks" over the years, because I felt like I should, or knew deep down that it would be helpful. However, after a couple of months (okay weeks; okay days!) those journals would inevitably end up on my office shelf with ample blank sheets. This book helped me solidify the "why" and also gave me enough of the "how" to re-engage my journaling efforts. Allison does a masterful job of weaving her personal narrative into the practice of journaling.

Jeff Shipman
Teaching Pastor, Columbia Crossroads Church; President, Christ Together Network

Journaling as a Spiritual Practice reflects the same depth of insight I have witnessed in Allison's teaching. Having journeyed through the book myself, I can attest to the skill with which she integrates psychological principles into her prompts. Along the way, there are moments of challenge and moments of renewal, times of emotional release and times of fresh strength. Allison has given us a gift in this book. It is a companion for the weary, a guide for the searching, and a tool for anyone longing to encounter healing through the practice of journaling. I commend it to you with great confidence, knowing that it will meet you wherever you are and lead you toward deeper wholeness.

Ken Kelly, MA, LPC, NCC

I first encountered Allison's journaling prompts at a retreat, and even as a lifelong journaler, they helped me recognize God's hand in my story from a new perspective. *Journaling as a Spiritual Practice* blends thoughtful prompts with Allison's own poignant story of pain, response, and healing. This book is a wonderful choice for anyone seeking to write with depth and hope.

Katy Rose
Artist and author, *Art for Joy*, *Miss Prim Goes Wild*, and *Lilibet the Brave*

As a writer and occasional journaler, I reluctantly walked into one of Allison's journaling sessions, almost certain I already knew all I needed to know. But that evening, I met another part of myself. It was as if Allison held my hand as I went deep inside and found the silenced places within me. My pen became a microphone, and journaling became an invitation for my soul to speak. That moment gave voice to the quiet corners of my heart, and through journaling, I began to hear and see myself in ways I never imagined. *Journaling as a Spiritual Practice* invites readers to do the same: to slow down, listen inwardly, and encounter God through the written word. This book is not just about writing; it is about spiritual renewal, healing, and rediscovering the holy presence of God within the pages of our own stories. I am overjoyed that through her new book, the world now gets a chance to experience that same renewal.

Victoria Harris-Thomas
Author of "The Becoming: A Lyrical Audiobook"

Every word dips your heart deeper into the grip of pain and doubt she so clearly struggled with. Just when you think you're in deep waters with her, she pulls you deeper still. Journaling with Allison's prompts can lead you back to this one profound truth, an awareness that God is here. Do your soul a favor and put pen to page with Allison Byxbe.

Angela Calabrese
Founder of Forever Changed Films; producer of *Sound Mind Series*

If you've ever had the joy of learning from Allison in a journaling class, this book feels like bringing her home with you! *Journaling as a Spiritual Practice* reminds me of sitting down for a meaningful conversation with a friend—one who asks just the right questions. Through her reflections and prompts, you'll discover new insights about yourself and learn how to let God's transformative presence flow through the simple act of putting pen to paper.

Michelle Robinson Trayers
Adult Discipleship Pastor at East Lake Community Church and Leadership Coach